CHARACTER COUNTS

An Interactive Bible Study

Character Counts
ISBN 978-0-7392-0319-4
Copyright 1998 by Cindy Miller
2010 Revised and Updated

All Scripture quotations in this book are from the New King James
Version of the Bible unless otherwise identified.

Cover Design:
Angela Carrington
Inspire Media, LLC

Published by
Classic Publishing
Dover, Delaware
www.myclassicpublishing.com

The latest rage in North America is to be a victim,
to blame others instead of taking responsibility for our own cowardly,
selfish, or lazy choices in life. It is time to stop making excuses
because contrary to popular opinion...

CHARACTER COUNTS

An Interactive Bible Study

A Revised and Updated Edition

Cindy Miller

CLASSIC
PUBLISHING
Dover, Delaware

Contents

Dedication

For my precious sons, Jonathan and Nathan,
men of strong character,
who fill my life with love and laughter.

With special thanks to Francy and Gina
who love me unselfishly
and more importantly
love the work of God.
Thank you for all the helps you bring to my ministry
and for making it so much fun.

Foreword

It seems only natural that Cindy Miller would author this book because she is a woman of many talents as well as a splendid role model for the subject of character. As a wise and effective manager of her time, she has written so that a busy person can use the book at intervals without losing the vital messages given.

Character Counts is more than facts and information. Rather, the study stimulates critical thought about who we really are. The issues in the book are timeless, especially as we realize the universal and historical vulnerability of humanity to sin. John reminded us of this, "For all that is in the world, the lust of the flesh, and the lust of they eyes, and the pride of life, is not of the Father, but is of the world" (I John 2:16).

I believe this study will influence your life now and for eternity. Now, in how you behave, make choices, and commit to God. Eternity in heaven by making character count. Though our social pressures may vary greatly, committing our-selves to the lessons taught here can yield the stable character so sorely needed in our world.

One final thought, Paul said in Colossians 3:16 that we were . . . "to let the Word of Christ dwell in you richly in all wisdom." This study will help you help yourself and others to put "first things first" by building strong moral character on a Biblical foundation.

Gwyn Oakes
President, Women's Division
United Pentecostal Church International

Preface

In the alphabet, the letter *C* comes before the letter *G*. In life, *Character* comes before *Gift*. Or it should. We live in a world that confuses personal ability or gifts with "good" and believes that charisma is more important than character. This is evidenced by the acceptance and admiration society lavishes on sports figures, movie stars, and politicians who live glamorous public lives while flaunting shameful behaviors.

Life is full of tough choices and <u>choosing to do right doesn't always feel good or bring quick rewards</u>. However, the basic tenet still remains true . . . it is always right to do right!

Albert Einstein once said, *"The most important human endeavor is the striving for morality in our actions. Our inner balance, and even our very existence, depends upon it. Only morality in our actions can give beauty and dignity to our lives."*

The concepts found in this book, when applied, will repair, redirect, and renew your life.

Cindy Miller

The Ingredients of Character

"It is better to be despised for the right
than praised for the wrong."

Does your word hold value?

Do you keep promises?

Do you "say what you mean and mean what you say"?

Are you loyal to your friends and family?

Do you obey God?

The word *character* has been defined as "the person you are when no one is looking".

Character is the makeup, traits, and quality of a person. Having values, morals, and integrity is what makes you a valuable spouse, parent, friend, co-worker, and neighbor.

Reflection

How am I valuable in my relationships?

There are old-fashioned words that define people with character – moral, ethical, honest, with a sense of fair play, value, integrity, and honor. These internal unseen components are reflected in choices, conduct, communication, and consistency. The internal becomes visible through a person's ability to fulfill life's demands, which come in the form of relationships, personal challenges, failures, problems, and the unexpected crisis in life. In all of this the ultimate test of character is in our answer to the question, do we reflect the image of God?

> When do you develop character?
> What is a conscience?
> Where do convictions come from?
> Why do you need courage?
> How does all this apply to Christian living?

Character is not an isolated quantity or a lone ingredient. Rather, character is made up of several entities.

- Conscience: our capacity to make right choices. An internal voice that guides us in decision-making processes.
- Convictions: a strong belief in what is good and right.
- Courage: the ability to sacrifice for your beliefs when doing wrong is easier, feels better, and brings a reward.

These three ingredients – conscience, convictions, and courage — make up character.

Reflection

Your character is reflected in the choices you make and the conduct that follows.

How Do You Recognize a Person Lacking In Character?

A person with little character is someone who cannot be depended on to do what is right. Individuals may "talk a good talk," but, in the moment of decision, may choose to serve selfish interests first and give the leftovers to those they claim to love. Does this sound like someone you would choose for a friend, a spouse, someone to co-parent your child? *Worse, does this describe you?*

Do you know someone who:
- Makes excuses for and justifies wrong behavior?
- Screams "victim" and collapses into an emotional wheelchair rather than take responsibility for immoral choices?
- Blames others for their own inappropriate conduct?
- Uses "but" statements to explain unreasonable emotions and decisions. "I know I got angry and overreacted, *but* she . . ."

People with little character jump on the bandwagon of blaming others instead of taking responsibility for their choices in life. A person lacking character repeatedly ignores and quiets that internal guiding voice that we call conscience.

In Shakespeare's Julius Caesar, Cassius forms a group of conspirators to kill Caesar because they feel he is a threat to the Republican form of government, which is also the foundation of their wealth and power. Caesar wanted to be crowned king, and would probably abolish the need for the senate, in essence, themselves. Most of the conspirators are friends or cohorts with Caesar and have added to his power and acceptance with the people. As Cassius convinces Brutus to join in the act of murder, he speaks a line that sums up how most people look at their lives:

> *"The fault, dear Brutus, is not in our stars,*
> *But in ourselves, that we are underlings."*
> *Act I, Scene ii, lines 140-141*

We often try to blame others, or fate, or something other than ourselves for our own life situations resulting from our own choices.

The Journey to Living Right

The journey to right relationships and right living starts by doing right things. *It is always right to do right*, and therein lies the secret to the true quality of life.

Humanistic psychologists have spent years saying that it is externals that are responsible for the problems in our lives. We have become a world of victims, crippled by the actions of others, condemned to spend the rest of our lives in emotional wheelchairs.

The Bible does not support this doctrine of victimization or support our feeble efforts to justify our lack of character by blaming others and events for our own cowardly, selfish, or lazy choices in life.

Being human is an awesome experience. We are not merely creatures living out a biologically controlled destiny, but we are creatures made in the image of God and empowered by His Spirit. This enables you to live a life of overcoming rather than accept an attitude of defeat. There is glory in overcoming!

There was a wise man that always had the right answers to some of life's tough problems. A young man approached him to ask a questioned designed to stump him. "Sir, is the bird in my hands alive or dead?" he asked. Of course, he planned that the old man would be proved wrong at all counts, for, if he said the bird was alive, the young man would simply squeeze the bird to death, and if he said the bird was dead, he would open his hand and how it was alive. The old sage looked at the young upstart and replied, "My son, it is whatever you wish it to be." (McHenry, 37)

As a human being you control your emotions. You choose your behaviors and in doing so, you decide your destiny. The philosopher, Archimedes, said, *"Give me a firm place to stand and I will move the earth."* Character is your firm foundation.

In order to have strong character, we must have deep convictions, a vociferous conscience, and a determined courage.

➤ TIME FOR RESPONSE

In an honest evaluation of your daily decisions, are you a person with good, little, or flawed character? _____

_____

How did you determine your answer?_____

_____

_____

Do you blame others instead of taking responsibility for your own life choices?_____

_____

Have you ever felt crippled or handicapped by an event or person in your life? How has this affected your life?_____

_____

Our character is the result of our free choices
– right or wrong – that we have made in life.
Do you agree or disagree?_____
Why?_____

_____

What are the weak areas of your life where your character is tested?_____

_____

What would need to change in order for you to become known as a person of strong character?_____

_____

*"A good name is to be chosen rather than great riches.
Loving favor rather than silver and gold"*
(Proverbs 22:1).

God's Principles
Vs.
Man's Philosophies

"Beware lest anyone cheat you through philosophy and empty deceit, according to the tradition of men, according to the basic principles of the world, and not according to Christ"
(Colossians 2:8).

The philosophies of this world entice us and have a magnetic pull because they sound so right and feel so good. Human philosophies promote a lack of personal guilt and create acceptability to blame someone or situations for our own lack of character.

The Garden of Eden was a perfect paradise, a place of perpetual springtime with blossoming fruit trees, colorful flowers, green grass, and lush plants. The only requirement God gave Adam and Eve was to not eat of the fruit from one tree in the garden (Genesis 2:16-17). Sadly, the temptation proved too great, and not only did the woman eat, but she shared the fruit with her husband. *"Then the eyes of both of them were opened…"* (Genesis 3:7). It wasn't that Adam and

Eve weren't informed about the tree or the consequences of disobedience. It was that, in a moment of crucial decision-making, they chose to satisfy self rather than do right and this was an abdication of character.

The Name of the Game is Blame ⊙ ⊙ ⊙ ⊙ ⊙ ⊙ ⊙ ⊙ ⊙ ⊙ ⊙ ⊙ ⊙ ⊙

In the cool of the day (Genesis 3:8-13), the Lord came and began to ask some tough questions that demanded a response. Human nature, now compromised from God-like-ness, did three things that are still done today.

In reading Genesis 3:7-13, we discover the three things Adam and Eve did in response to their sin:
- "And they sewed fig leaves together, and made themselves coverings" (verse 7).
- "And Adam and his wife hid themselves from the presence of the Lord God" (verse 8).
- "And the man said, 'the woman . . . gave me'" (verse 12); "and the woman said, 'the serpent deceived me, and I ate'" (verse 13).

Adam and Eve quickly learned to respond to guilt by *covering, hiding, and blaming.* Since that time, humans have used this handy little tool devised to get one off the hook when the consequences do not look inviting. What an easy trap to fall into. We are off the hook! No responsibility, no accounta-bility, no pressure, no demands. *So why isn't it working?*

**Moral perfection is impossible
but striving for moral excellence
is an attainable goal.**

Moral Excellence

Morals are in the mentality of mankind. How else can we explain what anthropologists refer to as universal taboos? We do not live in a one-world culture, yet universal rules do exist. For example, universally it is usually considered wrong to engage in or allow incestuous relationships. Even among the more liberal cultures that exhibit few sexual inhibitions, incest is not acceptable. Anthropologists are at a loss to explain this phenomenon, and while admitting that incest avoidance among humans is not biological, will only admit that any other convincing explanation of the taboo has still to be advanced. I would like to submit to anthropologists that morals are a part of the human make-up.

The ability to make choices is based upon man's special creation by God. Out of all of God's creative work, only man was made in the image of God. "So God created man in His own image; in the image of God He created him; male and female He created them" (Genesis 1:27). When the Bible tells us that we are made in the image of God, it wasn't referring to eye color or the size of our nose; rather it meant the God-like attributes that make up the souls of men. To reflect the image of God is to mirror His attributes, temperament, and attitudes. Therefore, to be fully human, we must take on Godliness or God-like-ness.

However, when we take on the characteristics of God and His value system, we find a new meaning to life, and people will sacrifice for whatever they value. God's value system and His character, along with the principles for a successful life, are fully explained in the Bible. In order to understand *character*, we must go back to the Bible and discover what it says about the importance of implementing these principles in our own lives.

What Is God-like-ness?

" Now may the God of peace Himself sanctify you completely; and may your whole spirit, soul, and body be preserved blameless at the coming of our Lord Jesus Christ"
(1 Thessalonians 5:23).

SPIRIT

BODY　　　　　　　**SOUL**

Here is the total picture of character development in God's eyes. His intention is that we be complete, whole, not fractured or out of balance. Each part of us is truly integrated – BODY, SOUL, AND SPIRIT. Often, we pay more attention to one part, and deprive the other of necessary nutrition and opportunity for growth. When that happens, we become out of focus and out of balance. What happens to us or in us impacts all of us.

Yet, we have access to a power greater than our own. We have a provision of helps that allow us to become more like Him. Godliness is within our reach.

"As His divine power has given to us all things that pertain to life and godliness, through the knowledge of Him who called us by glory and virtue, by which have been given to us exceedingly great and precious promises, that through these you may be partakers of the divine nature,"
(2 Peter 1:3-4).

Reflection

What is sin? Sin is thoughts and behaviors, which are contrary to the character of God. To sin is to commit an offense against God.

What Is Sin?

Today, the word sin is rarely used to describe human misbehavior. *Have we lost our ability to recognize sin? Do we feel the concept of sin is old-fashioned?* As Christians we must draw the line in a world of guilt-free living. Yet, is any sinner – unless hardened by sin – really living guilt free?

Abortion in Japan has been legal since 1948, and about 400,000 are performed each year. It would seem that the subject would not engender guilt. Yet, in a New York Times article it was reported that thousands of women visit Buddhist temples each year with a statuette personifying their destroyed fetus and bearing a name for the child. Some of the statuettes are clothed in hats, bibs, and hand-knit sweaters. Some women feel that what they have done is bad enough for them to be cursed.

Paul said in Romans 2:14-15a, that "for when Gentiles, who do not have the law, by nature do the things in the law, these, although not having the law, are a law to themselves: who show the work of the law written in their hearts, their conscience also bearing witness, and between themselves their thoughts accusing or else excusing them."

What is your conscience (thoughts) accusing or excusing in your life? When sin is present it is usually accompanied by an uncomfortable feeling we call guilt.

What Is Guilt?

Guilt is a feeling in response to a behavior, which contradicts God's Word, our own convictions, or society's code of conduct. God designed guilt to bring a sense of personal responsibility for behavior He considers sin.

The issues of sin must be dealt with if we are going to mirror the image of God.

" . . . *let us lay aside every weight, and the sin which so easily ensnares us, and let us run with endurance the race that is set before us . . .*"
(Hebrews 12:1).

The New International Version reads like this,
" . . . *let us throw off everything that hinders and the sin that so easily entangles, and let us run with perseverance the race marked out for us.*"

I prefer the word "*beset*" as used in the King James Version, *"the sin which doth so easily beset us,"* means harass, assail, surround. Sins that *beset* us should scream out a warning because they say that there is a lack of core values and convictions in our life, which reflect the neglect of character building. And, the sin that *besets* us should alert us to the fact that we have repeatedly ignored that still small voice we call conscience.

How Do We Change? ●

People want a quick fix. Instead of embarking on a journey of growth, maturity, and self-responsibility they desire life to be easy with few consequences. It is through that lens that children view life. When we grow up it means living as mature adults not immature children. It requires a higher standard of living.

How does a person change? Developing strong convictions and viewing life with a maturing mentality build character.

How does a person build character? By courageously implementing right. It is always right to do right and it is always wrong to do wrong.

How does a person know what is right? By discovering God's principles and making them your own; thereby, establishing a core value system.

What is the first step? Begin to listen to that inner voice and allow your conscience, which is being developed through the Word of God, to guide you. Adhering to values, morals, and ethics help prevent problems in life.

As Christians, we must be fully persuaded that our source of reference is the Bible. Then, we need to determine if our choices and conduct is consistent with the convictions we profess to adhere to.

➤ TIME FOR RESPONSE...

From the story in Genesis 3, list three responses Adam and Eve had to their sin:

_____

_____

_____

In what ways have you ever reacted like Adam and Eve in response to your own sinful behavior?_____

_____

_____

If you are playing the blame game, whom do you blame for the failures or problems in your life?_____

_____

_____

What choices have you made that surround you, harass you, and assault you? Did this happen because of lack of convictions in a particular area of your life or did it occur after ignoring your conscience?_____

_____

_____

What areas in your life are you not doing the right things even though you are fully aware of what right is?_____

_____

_____

Explore the areas of weakness in your life in honest evaluation and with a determination to change._____

_____

_____

*"Therefore, to him who knows to do good,
and does not do it, to him it is sin"*
(James 4:17).

Your *Conscience*: Listen To It

"The voice of conscience is so delicate that it is easy to stifle it; but it is also so clear that it is impossible to mistake it."

Our conscience is our ability to judge ourselves in moral terms as defined by the expectations of God, society, culture, and families. Since 1811, Uncle Sam has received anonymous sums of money as self-imposed fines for a variety of reasons. The first donation was in the amount of $5.00. The smallest donation was less than a dollar given by a woman who had reused stamps. Their reasons varied but the results were the same …they were all seeking relief from a guilty conscience. All these monies have been placed in an account named the Federal Conscience Fund that now totals over six million dollars. This fund is a result of a person's internal voice called conscience talking loud enough to produce an emotion of guilt that motivated restitution.

Reflection

**The greatest tormentor of the human soul
is a guilty conscience.**

What is This Thing Called Conscience?

One definition (Vine) is: "that process of thought which distinguishes what it considers morally good or bad, commending the good, condemning the bad, and so prompting to do the former, and to avoid the latter."

A closer look simplifies this definition into bite-sized thoughts.

1. The conscience is a process of thought.
2. The conscience has the job of distinguishing (make a distinction between).
3. The conscience evaluates and categorizes the morally good or bad.
4. The conscience, because of Biblical beliefs and core convictions, commends the good and condemns the bad.
5. The conscience prompts the listener to do what is right and avoid what is wrong.

A pure conscience is only possible when living in a relationship with Jesus Christ and sincerely pursuing His Truth in an effort to implement that Truth and live it out. A conscience must be biblically developed. Are your moral judgments made based on God's Truth or popular opinions? The Apostle Paul talked about *"love from a pure heart, from a good conscience, and from sincere faith"* (I Timothy 1:5).

Developing a Pure Conscience

We have the privilege of bringing every thought and belief before God for a review. The more we know Him, the more we know His Word, the more we live intentionally implementing what we know into our everyday lives, the stronger and healthier the voice of our conscience becomes. We must start listening to this inward voice that speaks as a guide. Then we can say, *"For our boasting is this: the testi-mony of our conscience that we conducted ourselves in the world in simplicity and godly sincerity, not with fleshly wis-dom but by the grace of God, ..."* (2 Corinthians 1:12).

In summary, we develop a pure conscience by:

1. Allowing God to review our thoughts, beliefs, and convictions for the purpose of correction. *"There-fore, since we through God's mercy have this ministry, we do not lose heart. Rather, we have renounced secret and shameful ways; we do not use deception, nor do we distort the word of God. On the contrary, by setting forth the truth plainly we commend ourselves to every man's conscience in the*

sight of God" (2 Corinthians 4:1-2, NIV).

2. Maintaining a daily interaction with God through prayer.

3. Consistently reading and pondering the Scriptures as a guide to life. *"For whatever things were written before were written for our learning, that we through the patience and comfort of the Scriptures might have hope"* (Romans 15:4).

4. Obeying God's correction and direction. *"Your word I have hidden in my heart, that I might not sin against You"* (Psalm 119:11).

Pure Conscience vs. Defiled Conscience ° ° ° ° ° ° ° ° °

The Bible also makes us aware that by ignoring our conscience and choosing to live according to our own will and pleasures we can defile the conscience. I Timothy 4:1-2 reads, *"Now the Spirit expressly says that in latter times some will depart from the faith, giving heed to deceiving spirits and doc - trines of demons, speaking lies in hypocrisy, having their own conscience seared with a hot iron."*

Reflection

What does it mean to "give heed to" deceiving spirits?

What Does The Bible Say? ⊛

"I myself always strive to have a conscience without offense toward God and men" (Paul in his defense before Felix, Acts 24:16). The NIV reads *"So I strive always to keep my conscience clear before God and man."*

What does *"offense"* mean? Offense is to offend, cause difficulty, discomfort, or injury – also, to spiritually transgress moral or divine law. Our goal as followers of Christ is two-fold:

1. Not to offend.
   "A brother offended is harder to win than a strong city, and contentions are like the bars of a castle" (Proverbs 18:19).
   Contemporary Version: *"Making up with a friend you have offended is harder than breaking through a city wall."*

   "...that you may be sincere and without offense till the day of Christ" (Philippians 1:10b).

2. Refuse to be offended.
   "Great peace have they which love thy law; and nothing shall offend them" (Psalm 119:165, KJV).

When an offense comes, and it will, we cover it by applying Scriptures to the situation that put it in perspective and help us to regain our equilibrium. Maturity demands a Godly response.

"Pray for us; for we are confident that we have a good con - science, in all things desiring to live honorably" (Hebrews 13:18).

Reflection

Our conscience is our ability to choose behaviors that conform to the principles and values that we have internalized and made a part of our inner being.

In John 8:1-9 we read an incredible story of the power of an active vociferous conscience. One morning Jesus went to the temple and soon a crowd began to gather. As Jesus sat teaching the people, the Jewish leaders and Pharisees interrupted. Disliking Jesus and looking for an opportunity to trump up charges against Him, they brought a woman to the front of the crowed and began shouting, *"Teacher, this woman was caught in adultery, in the very act. Now Moses, in the law command - ed us, that such should be stoned. But what do You say?"* Jesus stooped and wrote in the dust of the ground. This only aggravated the accusers, and they continued to press for an answer. Finally, Jesus rose and replied, *"He who is without sin among you, let him throw a stone at her first."* With that He went back to writing on the ground. *"Then those who heard it, being convicted by their own conscience, went out one by one, beginning with the oldest even to the last.*"

Have you ever been convicted by your own conscience? God has not called us to live perfect but He has called us to live responsibly. Maturity enables us to live aware of our constant need for a Savior.

➤ TIME FOR RESPONSE...

Like the men in the story told in John 8:1-9, have you ever been convicted by your own conscience?⎯⎯⎯⎯⎯⎯
⎯⎯⎯⎯⎯⎯⎯⎯⎯⎯⎯⎯⎯⎯⎯⎯⎯⎯⎯⎯⎯⎯⎯⎯⎯⎯

What concerns do you have about the development of your conscience? Do you feel your conscience is pure?⎯⎯⎯⎯
⎯⎯⎯⎯⎯⎯⎯⎯⎯⎯⎯⎯⎯⎯⎯⎯⎯⎯⎯⎯⎯⎯⎯⎯⎯⎯

What are you currently doing or willing to begin doing to "purify" your conscience so that it can be a trusted voice guiding you in the daily decisions of life?⎯⎯⎯⎯⎯⎯⎯⎯⎯⎯⎯⎯
⎯⎯⎯⎯⎯⎯⎯⎯⎯⎯⎯⎯⎯⎯⎯⎯⎯⎯⎯⎯⎯⎯⎯⎯⎯⎯

How does the Word of God "hidden in our heart" (Psalm 119:11) help our conscience?⎯⎯⎯⎯⎯⎯⎯⎯⎯⎯⎯⎯⎯⎯
⎯⎯⎯⎯⎯⎯⎯⎯⎯⎯⎯⎯⎯⎯⎯⎯⎯⎯⎯⎯⎯⎯⎯⎯⎯⎯

Read Proverbs 6:20-23. How does this relate to the work of the conscience?⎯⎯⎯⎯⎯⎯⎯⎯⎯⎯⎯⎯⎯⎯⎯⎯⎯⎯
⎯⎯⎯⎯⎯⎯⎯⎯⎯⎯⎯⎯⎯⎯⎯⎯⎯⎯⎯⎯⎯⎯⎯⎯⎯⎯

*"For when Gentiles, who do not have the law,
by nature do the things in the law, these, although
not having the law, are a law to themselves: who
show the work of the law written in their hearts, their
conscience also bearing witness, and between
themselves their thoughts accusing or else
excusing them."*
(Romans 2:14-15a)

Your *Convictions*: Act Upon Them

"The most important thing about a man is what he believes in the depth of his being. This is the thing that makes him what he is. The thing that organizes him and feeds him; the thing that keeps him going in the face of untoward circumstances; the thing that gives him resistance." Hugh Stevenson Tigner

There is a problem-plagued theory in our culture call non-judgmentalism, which preaches a no-fault, guilt-free living package. People are attracted to moral relativism because it justifies their behavior without having to think about their personal convictions or beliefs. It offers an escape from the necessity to think about and make decisions on such important matters as cheating, stealing, lying, and other moral issues. Someone once said, "Great men have convictions – ordinary men have only opinions." If great men have convictions, and ordinary men have opinions, what do people without convictions and opinions have?

Conviction has been so far removed from our lives that while, in a survey, some college students acknowledge the fact of the Holocaust, they will not bring themselves to say that killing millions of people is wrong. While these students may deplore what the Nazis did, their disapproval is expressed as a matter of taste or personal preference, not moral judgment. One student spoke for a multitude when he said, "Of course I dislike the Nazis, but who is to say they are morally wrong?"

Reflection

Dante said years ago "the hottest places in hell are reserved for those who, in a period of moral crisis, maintain their neutrality."

Jeffrey Dahmer committed horrible atrocities that were unthinkable to most Americans. However, one thing is certain. He had to lose a sense of value for life long before he killed his first victim. The psychologist who testified at his trial said, "he knew what he was doing, and he knew it was wrong". Dahmer demonstrates how important right convictions are to human beings. We often know when we are doing wrong; but as we cross the line of conviction, each transgression becomes easier.

You will not be popular when you stand strong in your convictions. The true test of character is having the courage to examine and/or change your convictions and conduct.

"I am tired of hearing about men with
the 'courage of their convictions'. Nero and
Caligul and Attila and Hitler had the courage of
their convictions . . . But not one of them had the
courage to examine their convictions or to change
them, which is the true test of character." Sidney Harris

The End Result

The word ABOMINATION is defined as "things utter-
ly repulsive". It appears several times in the Bible and is used
to reflect God's strong convictions about human misbehavior
known as sin.

What is the end result of choices made without conscience and conviction?

*"But the cowardly, unbelieving, abominable, murderers,
sexually immoral, sorcerers, idolaters, and all liars, shall have
their part in the lake which burns with fire and brimstone,
which is the second death"* (Revelation 21:8).

*"But there shall by no means enter it (heaven) any thing that
defiles, or causes an abomination or a lie:"*
(Revelation 21:27).

*"These six things the Lord hates, yes, seven are an abomina -
tion to Him: a proud look, a lying tongue, hands that shed
innocent blood, a heart that devises wicked plans, feet that are*

41

*swift in running to evil, a false witness who speaks lies, and
one that sows discord among brethren"* (Proverbs 6:16-19).

Walking The Walk ⊛

We assume that Christians should exhibit attitudes and
behave in a manner consistent with Biblical teachings. Yet, in
our own lives, we see many times that behavior does not fol-
low the attitude (or conviction) a person professes to believe.

I taught a series of lessons on this same topic in our
mid-week adult Bible study and asked for responses to the
question, "If you had 6 months to live, how would you spend
it?" Out of the 18 responses turned in, all but 1 mentioned
sharing the Gospel or witnessing. However, if sharing the
Gospel were a true attitude or conviction, our building would
not be able to hold our weekly visitors. So, while sharing the
Gospel is something we know all good Christians should do,
our lifestyle does not reflect this as a true conviction. Our attitude is not determining our behavior. Our beliefs about right
and wrong and appropriate behaviors and responses are put to
the test by reality.

The responses were thoughtful and reflective, showing
that the participants were probably living as close to their convictions as possible. Some responses displayed unrealistic
attitudes about Christianity by feeling that God requires a high
level of performance or perfection of us that is unachievable
and brings condemnation. One honest person forgot all the

spiritual elements of the class and cut straight to the priorities of her life. She wrote, "I would quit work, empty out my savings, and charge – charge – charge!" Most of the responses spoke of consistent prayer and Bible reading, of making things right with God, family, and others. If this is truly a conviction, then what are people waiting for? Why wait? Are there areas of your life where your convictions do not match your actions?

One of the problems facing Christians is that we have not taken ownership of the principles in the Word of God. We repeat certain key phrases or superficially adopt attitudes without buying the whole package. We hear the teachings, and we are able to parrot the proper responses; but we do not own the concept. People that borrow convictions are likely to say such things as "it's against my religious beliefs" or "my church doesn't allow us to do that". If these are your responses, the conviction isn't yours – you haven't taken ownership. So, when temptations or pressures unexpectedly arise, you may react according to your old nature or previous sinful habits, and not according to the convictions you profess to have.

"Conviction is worthless unless it is converted into conduct." Thomas Carlyle

Strength of Convictions ☀

There is a useful formula to remember how to enforce convictions: CONVICTIONS - BEHAVIOR - CONSISTENCY

What are the factors or conditions for Conviction-Behavior-Consistency?

1. The conviction must be strong and clear. Inconsistencies are found when convictions are weak and attitudes are unclear or unsettled. Anything that contributes to a strong conviction should increase Conviction-Behavior-Consistency.

One factor is the amount of information the person has about the conviction. To simply say, "I said so" doesn't give you understanding or want to. Is that why in Psalm 119:11 David said that he hid the Word in his heart so that he wouldn't sin against God? The New Testament writings to the church firmly instruct how Christians ought to live. They show us how to think, how to behave, and what to avoid in order to live a life pleasing to the Lord. This is the information that you must put in your life in order to determine your convictions.

I remember my aunt lecturing me that "caffeine isn't good for you," as I opened a diet coke for my morning breakfast. "Why not?" I asked, as I continued to pour the drink over ice. "I don't know, but it isn't," she admonished in her most "auntly" voice. But it wasn't until I read that excessive amounts of caffeine cause a toxic liver, creating a build up of estrogen and greater potential for breast cancer that my aunt's warning had any real impact on my thinking.

2. Another factor that strengthens attitudes is to rehearse and practice them.

Conviction-Behavior-Consistency is greater when people have to think about and express their attitudes. Maybe that is why the psalmist David was such a prolific writer. His written expressions of honest evaluation mixed with faith and hope strengthened his convictions.

3. A personal experience which requires an attitude change or the development of a conviction is more permanent than simply reading about it as an idea. So, Conviction-Behavior-Consistency will be greater when we have direct experience than if someone tells us about it.

4. We develop convictions from having a vested or selfish interest in the issue. It works for you!

If living for God saved your marriage, then you have a great conviction in the power of God to heal relationships. If you were healed of a physical ailment, then you have a strong conviction that God is a healer. If God provided in time of financial crisis, then you have a strong conviction that He will again provide if you have such a need.

> "Convictions are what we cling to
> in our lowest moment." Larry Crabb

Applying Your Convictions

Several studies have asked people whether they believe in God or consider themselves religious. Then, they were asked if they attended church. The results showed a very weak relationship between those who believed in God and the number that actually attended church. Behavior was not following conviction.

When a conviction is very strong, it does not have to be brought very forcefully to the person's attention to be strongly related to behavior.

Situational Pressures

We are influenced both by our convictions and by situations. When situational pressures are very strong, convictions are not as likely to determine behavior as when such pressures are weak.

Don't put yourself in situations where you will be tempted. For the single woman out on a date, a passionate moment is not the time to analyze your convictions regarding premarital sex.

What is a situational pressure? These pressures occur when experiencing coercion by way of influence by peers, co-workers, family, or society. Examples would include a teenager teased into doing what the group requires for acceptance or an employee covering up for the boss or a co-worker. When your need for approval or acceptance overrides your convictions, you are facing situational pressure.

Larry King, talk show host, related this incident from his childhood that shows how convictions can be wishy-washy. He and his friends love to play stickball, but it was hard to find a place to play. Many owners posted signs that said, "Private No Stickball Playing Allowed". King and his friends found a novel way to circumvent that direction, though, by putting in punctuation where they thought it was needed. Their rendering of the sign was: "Private? No! Stickball Playing Allowed."

Intents

What are our intentions in living this life and what do we intend to do for Christ? People who voice or write their intentions are usually more successful in carrying out the appropriate behavior. Why? Because we have thought through what we want and how to get there and the end result means more to us than the instant gratification that will last for a moment yet affect us for a lifetime.

It may be helpful to role-play a scenario you expect to find yourself and rehearse an appropriate response, so when you find yourself in the moment of decision-making you can lean on the script you have developed. Brainstorm numerous ways to respond to difficult challenges. Be prepared with an answer in the hour of temptation.

Owning Your Convictions

What are the areas of your life where you speak the Christian conviction but your behavior is not consistent with your belief/conviction? Do you talk the talk but not walk the walk?

To strengthen convictions:

1. Search the Scriptures for support in areas where you are tempted and yet you know that the action would not be pleasing to God. On index cards write down each Scripture that reaffirms your conviction/attitude and supports appropriate behavior. We need to establish consistency between our attitudes and our actions and live so that our behavior consistently reflects our convictions.
2. Rehearse. Carry your index cards with you every day and at every opportunity stop and read each index card out loud.
3. Remind yourself of the experiences that you have had that

created a need for behavioral change in your life. How was
this conviction/attitude developed?

4. <u>Role-play</u> the proper response in critical situations so that a
conviction is followed and not old habits. "If _____
happened then I would _____."

Reflection

-Convenient Convictions-
**Strong convictions still stand even if the situation
changes. Convenient convictions are when values about
sex, honesty, abortion, or truth become optional.**

➤ TIME FOR RESPONSE...

In your own words, briefly restate the four conditions for
Conviction-Behavior-Consistency. _____

_____

_____

_____

What are the areas of your life where you speak the Christian
conviction but your behavior is not consistent with your
spoken belief/conviction? Do you talk the talk but not walk
the walk?_____

_____

_____

When your value system is tested by opportunity, are you truly convinced in what you believe?_____

What are your convictions regarding the daily challenges and opportunities of life?_____

_____

_____

What are ways you can safeguard your good intentions to change?_____

_____

_____

_____

_____

_____

*"Therefore, my beloved, as you have always obeyed,
not as in my presence only, but now much more in my
absence… Do all things without complaining and disputing,
that you may become blameless and harmless, children of
God without fault in the midst of a crooked and perverse
generation, among whom you shine as lights in the world"*
(Philippians 2: 12,14-15a).

Your Courage: Activate It

"All right, they're on our left, they're on our right,
they're in front of us, they're behind us. . .
they can't get away this time."

Chesty Puller, when surrounded by 8 enemy divisions during WWII.

What is your perception of the situation? Courage is doing the right thing when your knees are knocking and you have no guarantee that right will bring a reward. Courage is not being totally devoid of fear; rather, it is about possessing more faith than fear. Why does a child of God need courage? It takes great courage to have faith in God when your faith seems misplaced. It takes great courage to live by the principles of the Word of God instead of the philosophies of men. It takes great courage to right a wrong. It takes great courage to overlook an offense. It takes great courage to forgive. It takes great courage to reconcile a relationship. It takes great courage to hold your peace. It takes great courage to boldly live for God. It takes great courage to obey God. Bold courage and constancy to purpose produces great results!

Remember the class I mentioned in the last chapter? Now it's your turn. If you knew you had six months to live, how would you spend the last six months of your life?

Now that you have had a few minutes to think about this question and jot down your first responses . . . what are you waiting for? Why wait to become more loving? Why wait to make peace with an enemy? Why wait to set your house in order? Why wait to share your faith with a neighbor? Why wait to make peace with God? Why wait to do those things that are necessary in order for you to leave behind a legacy of goodness, kindness, gentleness, and love?

Some things on your list are probably simple and easy to fit into your life, but you just haven't thought about it lately. Other things would only require that you make the change a priority instead of a "someday" item. Still, others might only demand that you slow down and work it into a busy schedule... things like: "play more with my children" or "take a long walk with my spouse and thank him for the years we've had together." Maybe now is the time to call a friend just to say, "Hello. I miss you."

For each of us there are a few items on our list that actually require something greater than reorganizing an over-loaded schedule . . . we need the courage to do it. We need courage to stand for truth at the risk of losing friends, family, and/or a career. We need courage to forgive, courage to change, courage to ask for forgiveness, courage to admit wrongdoing, courage to enact a behavioral change.

If you won't admit there is a problem – is there a problem? Wrong doesn't disappear because you are willingly blind.

Former first lady, Eleanor Roosevelt, remarked that, "You gain strength, courage, and confidence by every experience in which you really stop to look fear in the face. You are able to say to yourself, 'I lived through this horror. I can take the next thing that comes along.' You must do the thing you think you cannot do."

Reflection

Is there something in your life you think you cannot do?

Courage Defined

General Omar Bradley defined courage as "the capacity to perform properly even when scared to death."

John Wayne said, "Courage is being scared to death and saddling up anyway."

Andrew Jackson encouraged others with these words, "One man with courage makes a majority."

Webster's Dictionary defines courage as bravery.

The Bible gives us this wonderful promise: "Be strong and of good courage, do not fear or be afraid of them; for the Lord your God, He is the One who goes with you. He will not leave you nor forsake you" (Deuteronomy 31:6).

Courageous Men

Joseph could have been bitter about the betrayal of his brothers, a life of slavery, and what looked like empty promises, but he kept a right spirit and was reconciled with the very brothers who betrayed him (Genesis 37-45).

David could have been bitter when after being anointed king he had to flee for his life from Saul. Instead of ascending a throne, he was a man on the run. But he kept a right spirit and was called a "man after God's own heart" (I Samuel).

A wrong thought in our mind leads to a wrong attitude in our spirit and once that happens there is great potential for bitterness. Where does that initial wrong thought come from? A disappointment, an injustice, a false accusation, or a deep hurt.

The followers of Jesus were disappointed that He did not set up an earthly kingdom, and they were devastated by his death. So, while His followers wallowed in unmet expectations, a thief on a cross looked beyond his shame, recognized a Savior, and received a pardon and an eternal home in paradise.

Things are not always what they seem to be, but in our emotional perception of a situation . . . *before we give God time to act . . . when fear rules in the place of faith . . . when courage flees* – we can actually allow that wrong perception to travel from our mind to our heart and allow bitterness to set in.

During World War II, General George Patton was summoned by a military official who began raving about what a brave man General Patton was. General Patton interrupted him by saying that he did not consider himself to be brave but rather a coward. Later on in his biography he said this about courage and fear: "I learned very early in my life never to take counsel of my fears."

> "Courage puts a new
> face on everything." Emerson

What Does The Bible Say? ◦

"Have I not commanded you? Be strong and of good courage; do not be afraid, nor be dismayed: for the LORD your God is with you wherever you go" (Joshua 1:9).

"Wait on the Lord, be of good courage, and He shall strengthen your heart: wait, I say, on the Lord" (Psalm 27:14).

"Be of good courage, and He shall strengthen your heart, all you who hope in the Lord" (Psalm 31:24).

"Be strong, and of good courage; do not fear nor be dismayed" (I Chronicles 22:13b).

➤ TIME FOR RESPONSE...

Personalize Deuteronomy 31:6:

"Be strong and of good courage, do not fear nor be afraid of
_____*; for the Lord your God, He is the*
One who goes with you. He will not leave you nor forsake
you." Take those situations where you need to look fear in the
face and apply Deuteronomy 31:6 to it.

If you knew you had six months to live, how would you spend
the last six months of your life? What is in your life that will
require courage to change?————————————————

———————————————————————————

———————————————————————————

Choose a biblical story where the main character models grace
under pressure, forgiveness in the midst of evil, and choosing
right actions when wrong would have been easier and brought
a quicker reward. How does this story speak to you?————

———————————————————————————

———————————————————————————

———————————————————————————

Could it be that the crowd that screamed, "crucify Him," was
not a crowd of unbelievers, just cowards? (Mark 15) ————

———————————————————————————

———————————————————————————

———————————————————————————

———————————————————————————

———————————————————————————

Commitment to Character

Character does count.
It cannot be bought or sold – only acted upon.

Self-help books, while all the rage, are not a new thing. In 1859, Samuel Smiles published <u>Self-Help</u>, a book on how to succeed. Smiles believed "the spirit of self-help is the root of all genuine growth in the individual." I agree. All the knowledge in the world cannot change a person unless that individual truly wants to change.

What motivates a person to change? Usually, love or loss (pain) is what ignites the process of behavioral change. People who are successful in making changes:

1. Perceive change as a benefit.
2. Regarding lack of change as dangerous or detrimental.
3. Expect to actually change.

Stay focused on the person you want to become and behave in a way that is worthy of love and respect. Self-mastery and self-discipline are required for the building of character.

> **We will be known
> by the tracks that
> we leave behind.**
> **Dakota Proverb**

Having a strong, principle-centered character is not claiming perfection. It is, as Albert Einstein said, a life of striving for moral excellence in our actions.

What Is Transformation?

"And do not be conformed to this world:
but be transformed by the renewing of your mind"
(Romans 12:2a).

Transformation is a process that begins to take place when you begin to change your thought processes. Choices are no longer made based upon emotions because they are too unpredictable. Therefore, emotion cannot be the guiding force behind your behavior. There are times when emotions lie to us.

An immature person believes emotion is reality but a mature Christ-centered person turns to the principles of God's

Word to learn what a person of strong character would do. *"There are many plans in a man's heart, nevertheless the Lord's counsel-that will stand"* (Proverbs 19:21).

When the sorrows of life, death, doubt, loss, suffering, threat, conflict, loneliness, and rejection come – and they will – comfort yourself with the knowledge that while you may not be allowed to choose your situations, you are always allowed to choose your responses to them. Life is 10% what you make it and 90% how you take it. The word *crisis*, when written in Chinese, is composed of two characters. One represents danger and the other represents opportunity. Life's challenges can be stepping stones or stumbling blocks. It's your choice. A diamond is a chunk of coal that performed well under pressure.

A huge fire raged and the owner stood and watched his life's work disintegrate before his eyes. His loss was great because the property was only insured for $238,000, yet the damage was $2 million. He summoned his son with these words: "Find your mother and bring her here. She will never see anything like this as long as she lives." The next morning the man spoke to his employees and said, "There is great value in disaster. All our mistakes are burned up. Thank God we can start anew." And, 3 weeks later, Thomas Edison delivered his first phonograph!

It's up to us how we react to suffering – change or collapse.

Choices In Crisis ●

In a time of decision-making, you may want to ask yourself the following questions. You cannot answer based on emotion but with a *yes* or *no*. If the answer is *no* to any one question, then it is time to activate your courage, listen to your conscience, and make the right choices because character counts!

1. Do you think this is the right thing to do?
2. Would you want your spouse/child/friend to choose this behavior for their life?
3. Will acting upon this choice bring self-respect?
4. Will you keep the things that are worthwhile and valuable if you do this?
5. Will it make you be proud of your decision if this action ever becomes public knowledge?

Remember, it is decisions based upon character that determine your destiny. You will need:

● A strong vociferous conscience . . . listen to it.
● Core-value convictions . . . act upon them.
● Bold courage . . . activate it.
● A commitment to making wise choices.

> ### We write our own destiny.
> ### We become what we do.
> **Madame Chiang Kai-Shek**

Prayer ·

Dear Lord, I long to be a person of strong character. I ask that you create in me a clean heart and renew within me a right spirit. I give myself entirely to You. I offer to You all that I am and all that I hope to be. I yearn to walk in newness of life.

Thank You for awakening me to my need to build a strong character. I want to mirror Your image in all of my choices. I trust that you will be my helper as I grow and become all that I am capable of becoming. In Jesus' beautiful Name, amen.

➤ TIME FOR RESPONSE...

In what area of your life would you perceive change beneficial?_____

How will change benefit you?_____

Do you expect to actually change?_____

Why?_____

_____

What do you expect to occur if you **do not** institute the changes you see are needed? _____

_____

_____

Like Thomas Edison, have you ever found "value in disaster"?

_____

What is the disaster in your life that you were able to view as an opportunity?_____

_____

_____

What kind of person do you want to become? Choose a minimum of five adjectives that you want to define you. Using those adjectives, create a plan to implement the necessary emotions, thoughts, behaviors, and beliefs in your life in order for you to become the person you long to be.

_____

_____

_____

_____

_____

_____

"What lies behind us and what lies before us
are small matters compared to what lies within us."

Ralph Waldo Emerson